ISIAH THOMAS

BOBBY McDERMOTT

GRANT HILL

DAVE DeBUSSCHERE

JOE DUMARS

DAVE BING

DENNIS RODMAN

GEORGE YARDLEY

BOB LANIER

BILL LAIMBEER

WALTER DUKES

JERRY STACKHOUSE

CREATIVE ☾ EDUCATION
AARON FRISCH

Published by Creative Education, 123 South Broad Street, Mankato, MN 56001

Creative Education is an imprint of The Creative Company.

Designed by Rita Marshall

Photos by Allsport, AP/Wide World, Rich Kane, NBA Photos, SportsChrome

Library of Congress Cataloging-in-Publication Data

Frisch, Aaron. The history of the Detroit Pistons / by Aaron Frisch.

p. cm. – (Pro basketball today)   ISBN 1-58341-097-X

1. Detroit Pistons (Basketball team)–History–

Juvenile literature. [1. Detroit Pistons (Basketball team)–History.

2. Basketball–History.] I. Title. II. Series.

GV885.52.D47 F75 2001   796.323'64'0977434–dc21   00-047340

First Edition 9 8 7 6 5 4 3 2 1

DETROIT, MICHIGAN, STARTED OUT AS A TINY

FRENCH FORT IN 1701. IT BECAME SUCH A KEY SITE

for fur trading that French and British armies and Native American

bands fought many battles to gain control of it over the years. By the

early 1900s, the fort had grown into a city, and the fur trade had been

replaced by a booming automobile industry.

Detroit is today known as the "Motor City" and the "Automobile

Capital of the World," because it is the home of America's three big car

manufacturers—Ford, General Motors, and Chrysler. Since 1957, the city

has also been the proud home of a National Basketball Association

BOBBY McDERMOTT

(NBA) team. Given Detroit's business in building cars and car parts, it was only fitting that that franchise was named the Pistons.

{THE FORT WAYNE YEARS} The Pistons franchise actually started out in Fort Wayne, Indiana, in 1937. The team played in a small, industrial league under the owner-ship of Fred Zollner. Zollner owned a factory that manu-factured pistons for automobiles, so coming up with a name for the franchise was easy.

The Fort Wayne Pistons went 15–9 before losing the **1942** NBL title to the Oshkosh All-Stars.

In 1941, the Pistons joined the National Basketball League (NBL), one of the first professional leagues. Fort Wayne soon dominated the NBL, winning the league championship in 1944 and 1945 behind the leadership of star guard Bobby McDermott. But when the NBL and another pro league merged to form the NBA in 1949, the Pistons stopped running so smoothly. In its first five NBA seasons, Fort Wayne

GRANT HILL

Star forward George Yardley sparked the Pistons' offense in the mid-**1950s**.

GEORGE YARDLEY

finished near the middle of its division.

The team's luck finally changed for the better in 1954, when Zollner hired Charlie Eckman—a former NBA referee—as the Pistons' new head coach. With Eckman guiding such talented players as forward George Yardley and guards Max Zaslofsky, Andy Phillip, and Frankie Brian, Fort Wayne raced to the Western Division championship in 1954–55. Then, in the playoffs, the hard-charging Pistons beat the Minneapolis Lakers before losing in the NBA Finals to the Syracuse Nationals in a thrilling seven-game series.

Averaging 17 points a game, bruising center Larry Foust helped Detroit go 43–29 in **1954–55**.

The Pistons almost won the NBA title again the next year, losing to the Philadelphia Warriors in the Finals, but Zollner had a difficult decision to make after the season. The fans in Fort Wayne loved their team, but Zollner didn't think that the Pistons could compete for long

LARRY FOUST

Forward
Christian
Laettner dis-
played old-
fashioned
fundamentals
in the late **'90s**.

CHRISTIAN LAETTNER

in such a small city. So, the Pistons said good-bye to Fort Wayne and

moved to Detroit.

{FROM DeBUSSCHERE TO BING} The move
seemed to hurt the team, which posted losing records
year after year in Detroit. During that time, the Pistons'
lineup featured such fine players as forwards Walter
Dukes and Bailey Howell, guard Gene Shue, and young

swingman Dave DeBusschere. Of these, DeBusschere was the soul of the

team. Even though he was a fine scorer, he was better known for his

defense, rebounding, and intelligence. The Pistons were so impressed

with DeBusschere's leadership that, in 1964, they made the 24-year-old

both player and coach.

DeBusschere continued to star as a player, but he struggled as a

coach. The Pistons remained among the worst teams in the NBA, finish-

WALTER DUKES

ing last in the league in 1965–66 with a 22–58 record. After that season,

Detroit was given the second overall selection in the 1966 NBA Draft.

The Pistons wanted forward Cazzie Russell out of the nearby University

of Michigan, but after the Knicks took Russell with the top pick,

Detroit settled for a guard named Dave Bing.

When Bing arrived in Detroit, he knew that fans had hoped to get

Russell instead. But the 6-foot-2 guard quickly won those fans over with

his great hustle and knack for scoring. Although he wasn't physically

powerful or a particularly great shooter, Bing became the

team's top offensive weapon.

As a rookie, Bing scored 20 points per game and was

named NBA Rookie of the Year. The next season, he

became the first guard in two decades to lead the league

Behind Dave DeBusschere, the Pistons exploded for a club-record 118 points a game in **1967–68**.

in scoring. "You can't open up a man's chest and look at his heart," said

legendary Boston Celtics coach Red Auerbach. "But I guarantee there's

one big [heart] beating in Bing. Give me one man like Dave Bing, and I'll

build a championship team around him."

Unfortunately, the Pistons were never able to do that. The team

made the playoffs after the 1967–68 season but struggled the next year

after trading DeBusschere to the New York Knicks. DeBusschere went

BOB LANIER

on to help the Knicks capture two NBA championships, while the

Pistons sank to the bottom of the league standings again.

{LANIER DRIVES THE PISTONS} In 1970, Detroit again looked

to the NBA Draft to find the answer to its problems. That year, the

Pistons picked a young center named Bob Lanier. Lanier gave the team

another capable scorer, but—at 6-foot-11 and a muscular 275 pounds—

his real calling card was his power. When Lanier went into the lane to get

a rebound, his opponents usually ended up empty-handed and battered

for their effort.

"I was well aware of Bob's great strength," said

Cleveland Cavaliers center Steve Patterson after battling

Lanier for a rebound. "But . . . I hammered him, and I

practically hung on him. Then, all of a sudden, he just

wrapped his arm around me and threw me to the ground like I was

made of straw. . . . I still don't know how he did it."

With Lanier's muscle added to their attack, the Pistons rose in the

standings over the next few seasons. In 1973–74, under new coach Ray

Scott, they jumped to a 52–30 mark and made the playoffs for the first

of two straight seasons. Sadly, those would be the Pistons' last good sea-

sons for a long time.

Dave Bing's nonstop hustle and high-pressure defense made him a six-time All-Star.

DAVE BING

With 9,430 career boards, Bill Laimbeer became Detroit's all-time leading rebounder.

In 1976, Detroit bid farewell to Bing, trading him to the

Washington Bullets. Then, over the next five years, the Pistons hired and

fired several coaches as they sought the right leadership.

Nothing seemed to work. In 1979, the team traded Lanier

to the Milwaukee Bucks, and Detroit plunged to 16–66.

The Pistons desperately needed a hero.

{DETROIT RISES AGAIN} Detroit found that hero

in the 1981 NBA Draft, selecting point guard Isiah Thomas. The 6-foot-1

Thomas had just led Indiana University to the NCAA championship as

a sophomore, and the Pistons believed that he could carry them to the

top as well. "I believe God made people to perform certain acts," said

Will Robinson, Detroit's assistant general manager. "Frank Sinatra was

made to sing, Jesse Owens was made to run, and Isiah Thomas was

made to play basketball."

KELLY TRIPUCKA

In 1983, the Pistons brought in Chuck Daly as the team's new head coach. Over the next few seasons, Daly and general manager Jack McCloskey assembled a talented lineup. Thomas controlled the ball, for-

ward Kelly Tripucka led the team in scoring, and rugged center Bill Laimbeer controlled the boards. Sharpshooting guards Joe Dumars and Vinnie Johnson received few headlines but played big roles as well.

The Pistons clearly had talent, but equally impressive was their hustling style of play. Coach Daly preached an aggressive defense, and the

The Pistons' feared defense included forward John Salley, who blocked 125 shots in **1986–87**.

Pistons were so effective at double-teaming the ball that it often seemed like they had six or seven men on the floor. Usually guarding the opposing team's best offensive player was forward Dennis Rodman, who used his quick feet and wiry frame to become one of the NBA's best defenders.

In 1986, the Pistons traded Tripucka and another player to the Utah Jazz for high-scoring forward Adrian Dantley. With Dantley's addition, the team soared to 52–30 and reached the Eastern Conference Finals. Although Detroit then fell to the Boston Celtics, Coach Daly believed his team was ready to win it all. "We are going to accomplish something this franchise has never had," he told reporters and Pistons fans. "An NBA championship."

JOHN SALLEY

Guard Isiah Thomas led Detroit in assists for 13 consecutive seasons.

ISIAH THOMAS

{MOTOR CITY MADNESS} In 1987–88, the Pistons nearly made good on that promise, losing to the Los Angeles Lakers in seven tough games in the NBA Finals. The next season, Detroit would not be denied. The Pistons went 63–19 and breezed through the playoffs to meet the Lakers once again in the NBA Finals. This time, the Pistons swept the Lakers in four games behind the hot shooting of Dumars. The versatile guard, often overlooked because of his quiet nature, exploded for more than 27 points per game during the series.

Joe Dumars's sweet shooting and great defense carried Detroit to its first NBA title in **1989**.

"Dumars wouldn't miss," said Mitch Kupchak, a former NBA player and the Lakers' assistant general manager. "We kept waiting for him to miss. You could feel the whole building waiting. But it was as if he had forgotten how. He was scary."

For good measure, the Pistons repeated as NBA champs the next

JOE DUMARS

season, beating the Portland Trail Blazers in the Finals. Detroit was eager

to make it three championships in a row, but it was not to be. For several

years, the rugged Pistons had beaten up on the high-flying Chicago Bulls

in the postseason. But in the 1991 playoffs, the Bulls proved that they

had become the stronger team, ending Detroit's run.

The Pistons struggled over the next few seasons. They kept the core of the team—including Thomas, Laimbeer, Dumars, and Rodman—together, but they were no longer a contender. In 1992–93, the Pistons went 40–42 and missed the playoffs for the first time in 10 years. A year later, the team's glorious era officially came to a close. Rodman was traded to San Antonio, and Laimbeer and Thomas retired.

{STARTING ANEW} After all of the changes, only Dumars remained from Detroit's championship era. The Pistons knew that he would need a talented teammate or two to keep them afloat. In the 1994 NBA Draft, they found one, adding multitalented forward Grant Hill, who had led Duke University to two NCAA championships during his college career.

Hill had a big impact on the NBA in his first season. The rookie paced Detroit with nearly 20 points per game and led the league in

Dennis Rodman was named NBA Defensive Player of the Year in **1989–90** and **1990–91**.

27

DENNIS RODMAN

All-Star voting, beating out even Bulls superstar Michael Jordan. But Hill

didn't carry the Pistons by himself. Helping him was the ageless Dumars

and sharpshooting young guard Allan Houston. Even

though the Pistons finished just 28–54 that year, they

were clearly revving up.

Under new coach Doug Collins, the Pistons leaped to a

46–36 mark and a playoff berth the next season. Leading

the way again was Hill, who finished the year with an NBA-high 10

triple-doubles (posting at least 10 points, rebounds, and assists in a

game). "He shows up and he goes hard," said Dumars of his teammate.

"He is going to continue to be great for the next 10 years. The best is

yet to come."

The Pistons brought in two key additions in 1997, trading for

swingman Jerry Stackhouse and signing free agent center Brian

ALLAN HOUSTON

Williams. These players, along with Hill, Dumars, and guard Linsey

Hunter, gave Detroit a formidable lineup. But the team struggled for

wins, and Coach Collins was fired late in the season.

In 1999, Dumars retired and took a front office

position with the Pistons. Upon his retirement, the league

created the Joe Dumars Trophy, which would be awarded

each year to the player who best exemplified sportsman-

ship. "Joe Dumars represents the best of the NBA," said league deputy

commissioner Russ Granik. "Throughout his 14-year career, Joe carried

himself with dignity and integrity and showed that one can be both a

great athlete and a great sportsman."

The Pistons missed Dumars in 1999–00, but they still battled to a

respectable 42–40 record. They also found a new force in reserve for-

ward Jerome Williams, who led the team in rebounding. Unfortunately,

Ball-hawking guard Linsey Hunter paced Detroit in steals in both **1998–99** and **1999–00**.

LINSEY HUNTER

Speedy swing-man Jerry Stackhouse emerged as the Pistons' new offensive leader in **2000–01**.

JERRY STACKHOUSE

Forward
Ben Wallace
was the latest
in a long
line of great
Pistons
rebounders.

BEN WALLACE

after the season, the Pistons lost their franchise player when Hill left to

join the Orlando Magic as a free agent. The loss was a heavy one, but

Detroit soon signed another free agent—hardworking forward Joe Smith—to fill the void.

Since their days in the NBL, the Pistons have won four league championships. Although they have also experienced their share of down seasons, the Pistons have

always made their fans proud with their tough style of play. With the

continued backing of the Detroit faithful, today's Pistons hope to make

the Motor City the basketball capital of the world once again.

Detroit fans hoped that young point guard Mateen Cleaves would become the next Isiah Thomas.

MATEEN CLEAVES